AN IMPERFECT BOOK

Baman Tadiwala

Dedication

Mummy, Daddy, Mumma, Papa
&
To all the people who bring positive vibes.

1

Someone knocked you down
and you thought it was their strength?
For ages have passed,
but you ain't awake?

2

But that's the most beautiful thing about pain-
When you submit, it's your enemy.
When you don't, it's your friend.

3

The spirit in you says you can.
Body says you can't.
Accept.

4

You don't know the fighter in you
because even on your worst day
you're still the best.
Only if you believe.

5

You lost
and it brought disappointment to a few people.
They might have lost faith in you
but that's okay.
You need to accept their decision
and look up to those
who still proudly stand in your corner.
They are the ones who really believe.
These people have not given up on you
and so you will not give up on them!

6

If you win,
you live to tell a tale.
If you lose,
you can guide.
If you lose and then win,
you end up with an adventure.
You're never at a loss!

7

What can be more inspiring that you,
pushing yourself so hard
and saying,
"One more time!"

8

You're your own warrior
and this is your battle;
where you either bleed to win,
or you surrender and regret.

९

True test of your character is
not when you rise and stay grounded.
It's when your back is against the wall;
you shed a tear or two,
you stand up with a belief
that you will figure it out.

10

When things won't work,
your dream will tell you that
you've been smart enough,
but not brave!

11

...and that you should believe-

dreams never die!

They just grow at their time.

11

12

Success is like a sea.
Can it be ever chased at once?
Sometimes all you can do is wait
at the shore and believe,
that one day an opportunity
will come in form of tide
and take you away as ebb.

13

Today you've words
and people don't understand.
Tomorrow you may have a story
and still they won't care.
This shouldn't stop you
because you've come all the way from
broken words to create a beautiful story,
only meant for you to be lived
and appreciated!

14

Native source of diamond is coal.
Oh my dear,
you're not less than gold.

15

Life is a joy of giving.
And sometimes
joy of not giving a damn to all the negative vibes.

16

It hurts when someone is your universe
but you're just a part of their universe.

17

A 'zero' before a number is not considered,
but it becomes valuable
once it starts following a number.
In the same way,
you won't be valued before chasing your dream.

18

A dirty water rising up
and reflecting different colors of a fountain
also looks beautiful,
but you're avoiding all the gatherings
thinking you're not.
It's never about the beauty,
it's all about the confidence.

19

Before your failure makes peace with your present,
defeat it and move on!

20

Suffering said:
There is a big void in my heart,
can't you see?
For love is a word of past.
I hope you understand what I mean?

Strength replied:
No I don't see a void,
for light can only pass through it.
I sail in the fluid of your dark,
I hope you understand what I mean.

21

Everyone has a right to reject you
but no one has a right to stop you.

22

Look.
Deep in her eyes
she says yes!
Let's first achieve our dreams,
everything else can wait.

23

Dear Dam,

I'm not so sweet.
But you should know one thing;
that unlike you,
I'm not gonna dry away any time soon.

In case if you need me,
Ocean.

24

It's up to you.
Your cries can become your agony
or your song.

25

She was just a word in his dictionary.
No.
That word was not LOVE.
That word was HOPE!

26

Some people might come and leave,
and your life will change;
but it won't stop.

27

You're not the purest form of metal.
You're indeed an atom
and it has the power to make everything.

28

If you really love someone,
you work.
Because you know that
love is just not enough.

29

You don't see the difference!
You either come out as a strong person
or you get carried away to a different place;
only if you face the storm,
only if you stay.

30

Everyone has to go one day,
but that's not important.
What you do till you're here
and for what you'll be remembered,
that's important.

31

Once you become the master of your mind,
the masterpiece within you will come.

32

Someone cheated you
and it was not in your hand.
For you've been cheating yourself since then,
what about that?

33

No matter what the journey,
if you stand by your dreams
then your dreams will stand by you.

34

God has not written your script.
God has only given pages.

35

...and there is nothing more beautiful
than you respecting her thoughts
and she respecting your feelings.

36

It's always good with good people
and I know you're the best.
If your intentions are good
and if the path is correct,
then only you can stop yourself.

37

To walk alone on your path is difficult
but just think for a second,
in case if you succeed;
the path will no longer be unknown.

38

Chase a person who teaches you
how to chase your dreams!

39

When I close my eyes
I want to be with a person
who makes me realize
what it is to be like in present!

40

It's never about forgiving or forgetting your enemies.
somethings the real strength is ignoring 'em
when it matters the most!

41

Some people stay in the moment
and pass their whole life,
while others take it as challenge
to create again.

42

You're here,
living and breathing
because this place needs you here
to make it more beautiful.

43

It's your talent that brought you here
but it's your passion that will keep you going.

44

Chase like a Cheetah.
Run like a Deer.
Sing like a Cuckoo.
Live like a Lion.

44.5

Defeated by situation.
Winner by a choice.
Now, that's you. Isn't it ?

45

You don't have a license
and you want to break the rule?
Of course you can,
if you're the rule.

46

You don't need anything
except a very strong reason.

47

Do a favor to yourself,
Love someone who only loves you back.

48

Others will say, you lost.
But for someone who loves you,
you lost but you fought!

49

Embrace your pain and fight your fears
before someone teaches you,
how to cry!

50

You can overcome any fear by subtle approaches.
But what about fear of love?
Well,
You need a person for that,
and for that you need to trust someone
again!

51

After every night there is a day.
If not yesterday, today!

52

The truth is
everyone wants to talk about night
but no one wants to walk in darkness.

53

Move-on(verb):
When pain becomes the reason,
not an excuse.

54

Shattered into many pieces?
Well,
that's how you'll begin again-
piece by piece.

55

Time changes for everyone.
You're weak when your tears hide you.
You're strong when you hide your tears.

56

Game over!
And the small kid shifted to an other game.
Over!
And an adult committed suicide.

57

It's very important to celebrate small victories;
go on a lone date and give yourself a treat
because everyone will be there
when you do something big.

58

Perception matters a lot.
Adding water to milk is cheating.
Adding ice to soft drink is swag.

59

As you proceed ahead in your life,
the amount of difficulties are going to increase
It's like when you march towards the sun
you face more heat.
But then,
You can only go towards the sun
when you're capable.

60

Because most of the st
ories are worth telling.
Yours will be worth living.
Only when you write!

61

We're water in the water bottle.
A bottle has an expiry date,
not the water inside it.

62

Something which we are facing
others are facing in much brutal way.
World is full of flaws;
Some here, some there.

Deep inside this heart
there is a fear to fail.
A picture of victory in mind,
that's how all begin.

A reason to stop and take some rest.
All days are not the same,
so why this shame?
But to get up and continue the race,
isn't that a real chase?

63

There are stars
much brighter than our own sun.
They don't shine
'cause they are far away from us.

64

When you love someone
you never leave.
When you love someone
you stay.

You rise in their success
and give a hand when they fail.
Cross the roads together
and also walk on footpath, if needed.
When you love someone
You stay.

A business class seat
or just a backseat.
Still you never complain
because you know you've your place.
When you love someone

65

You've been ignored
because you're nothing for anyone.
Though, this universe doesn't ignore you
and at every step it gives you a chance
to prove that you never deserve to be ignored.

66

A man was forcefully submerged
into a pool of water.
Not knowing how to swim,
he haphazardly moved his hands
and turned his body here and there.
The only vision he had at that moment
was to live!
That, my friend, is called 'burning desire'.

67

You're a seed
and soil is your family.
Water that you get is the knowledge,
while sunlight is your Karma.

68

It doesn't matter
where you come from.
No one even cares
where you're heading.
So when it's your journey
and only you know the destination,
then why to stop?

69

You need to make settlement
with you withered pieces
as soon as possible
before someone uses them
to build their empire.

70

Sometimes when people push you over the line
you have to fight fire with fire
and come out as strong as steel.

71

People who are jealous of you
will one day form a group
and try to isolate you from their events.
At that time instead suffering
or crying out of pain,
make a promise to yourself
that this time will also change.

72

A man and a house
are often viewed more
when broken
or newly built.

73

The bruises of your defeat
are no way shameful and ugly.
They live to tell a story
of how a dream was over
but you were not finished.

74

Dirty like a puddle-
It was a fun to play.
Shallow like a pond-
It had to dry.
Fast like a river-
so had a little hope to unite.
Deep like an ocean-
and it stayed.

75

It's something about the passion
we all are so unaware.
Mondays are never hated
nor Sundays are over loved,
if you love your work.

76

When the oil in the lamp
is about to end,
it burns so fast and bright.
In the same, my dear friend,
the darkness around you
which is becoming more dense
is just about to end.

77

Sir,
I hope you realize this thing one day
that you've missed so many flights
while waiting for your train.

By the way sir,
A customer has just cancelled
his seat and this is the last flight
for today.
It will cost some
extra bucks, but I can make it
up for you, only if you wish? Do you?

78

To fray away your demons
you need to be a daredevil.

79

In the end no matter what anyone says;
you know you're beautiful
and you're so brave.
It's just that you look more awesome
when you don't give up.

Hey you!
Did you like the book?

If YES then please give a genuine
review on Amazon.

If NO then too I'm ready to hear
your criticism by your
valuable feedback.

And let's get connected…
Do see my write-up account on Instagram
@a_writer_from_india

9 789353 216771